How to Negotiate a Better Salary for Software Engineers

A Step-by-Step Guide to Negotiating a Higher Salary in the Software Engineering Industry

The Fix-It Guy

Table of Contents

Introduction

Hey there, ambitious software engineers, coding wizards, and tech enthusiasts! Are you tired of putting in endless hours of hard work, only to find your paycheck doesn't quite match your skills and expertise? Do you ever wonder if there's a secret handshake to unlock the door to a higher salary in the software engineering industry? Well, guess what? You've just stumbled upon the key, and it's not hidden in some obscure corner of the internet, it's right here, in your hands.

Imagine a world where your talents are not just recognized but celebrated, where your paycheck reflects the value you bring to the table. Picture yourself confidently striding into negotiations, armed with knowledge, charisma, and a winning strategy. No more settling for less than you're worth. No more feeling like the underdog in the salary game. It's time to flip the script and rewrite your story.

Welcome to "How to Negotiate a Better Salary for Software Engineers: A Step-by-Step Guide to Negotiating a Higher Salary in the Software Engineering Industry." This isn't just another self-help book; it's your ticket to financial empowerment, a roadmap to turning those zeros in your paycheck into heroes. Whether you're a fresh graduate stepping into the professional arena or a seasoned developer looking to climb the career ladder, this book is your trusty companion, your mentor, and your cheerleader.

Prepare yourself for a journey packed with eye-opening insights, practical strategies, and a sprinkle of humor because, let's face it, negotiating your salary shouldn't feel like a root canal, it should be empowering, exciting, and maybe a little bit exhilarating. In the pages that follow, we'll demystify the art of negotiation, break down the barriers that hold you back, and equip you with the tools to command the salary you deserve.

Get ready to dive into real-life scenarios, success stories, and expert advice that will transform you from a salary negotiation amateur into a confident, strategic negotiator. So, grab your favorite drink, find a cozy spot, and let's embark on this transformative journey together. By the time you put this book down, you won't just be armed with knowledge; you'll be armed with confidence, ready to take on the world, one salary negotiation at a time.

Buckle up, dear reader. Your journey to a better salary and a brighter future starts now. Let's make those dollar signs reflect your true worth!

Chapter 1

Preparing for the Negotiation

Researching Salary Benchmarks in the Software Engineering Industry

Welcome to the first chapter of your salary negotiation journey! If you're embarking on the quest for a higher salary, it's essential to start with a solid foundation. In this section, we'll delve into the crucial task of researching salary benchmarks in the software engineering industry. This step is akin to finding the North Star in your negotiation adventure, it provides you with a clear direction and helps you navigate the vast sea of salary figures.

Why Researching Salary Benchmarks is Crucial:
Understanding the salary landscape in your industry is pivotal for several reasons:

1. Setting Realistic Expectations: Researching benchmarks allows you to set realistic salary expectations based on your skills, experience, and location. It prevents you from aiming too high or settling for less than you're worth.

2. Knowledge is Power: Armed with accurate data, you enter negotiations confidently, ready to counter any lowball offers with facts and figures. Employers are more likely to take you seriously when you can demonstrate that your expectations are grounded in industry standards.

3. Negotiating Your Value: Research empowers you to articulate your value effectively. By comparing your skills and experience to industry averages, you can make a compelling case for the salary you desire.

How to Research Salary Benchmarks:

1. Online Salary Platforms: Explore reliable websites like Glassdoor, Payscale, and LinkedIn Salary Insights. These platforms provide detailed salary data specific to software engineering roles, considering factors such as experience level, location, and company size.

2. Industry Reports: Keep an eye out for industry-specific reports published by reputable organizations or consulting firms. These reports often offer in-depth analysis, highlighting trends and average salaries within the software engineering sector.

3. Network with Peers: Engage with fellow software engineers in your professional network. Discussing salaries (anonymously, if needed) can provide valuable insights into what your peers are earning, especially if they have similar qualifications and experience.

4. Consider Cost of Living: Salaries vary significantly based on the cost of living in different regions. Take this into account when comparing salaries. A higher salary might seem impressive, but it might not stretch as far in an area with a high cost of living.

Analyzing and Using the Data:
Once you've gathered salary data, analyze it thoroughly. Identify the average salary range for your role, considering your experience level and location. Use this information to set your baseline salary expectations. During negotiations, if the offered salary aligns with industry standards, you can focus on other aspects of the job, such as benefits and career growth opportunities. If the offer falls below the benchmark, you have a strong argument for why you deserve a higher salary.

Assessing Your Own Value and Skills

In your quest for a better salary, one of the most critical steps is understanding your value within the context of the software engineering industry. In this section, we'll explore the art of self-assessment, how to recognize your unique skills, experiences, and accomplishments and translate them into a compelling case for a higher salary.

Why Assessing Your Value Matters:

1. Self-Confidence: Knowing your worth boosts your confidence. Confidence is contagious and can leave a lasting impression during salary negotiations. When you believe in your value, others are more likely to believe in it too.

2. Strategic Positioning: By understanding your strengths, you can strategically position yourself in the job market. Highlighting your specific skills and expertise can make you a desirable candidate, setting the stage for more substantial salary offers.

3. Personal Growth: Self-assessment is not just about salary negotiation; it's also a tool for personal growth. Recognizing your strengths and areas for improvement empowers you to focus on continuous skill development, enhancing your value over time.

Steps to Assess Your Value and Skills:

1. Identify Your Key Skills: Make a list of your technical skills, programming languages, software tools, and any other expertise relevant to your field. Consider both hard skills (quantifiable abilities) and soft skills (communication, teamwork, leadership).

2. Evaluate Your Experience: Reflect on your work experience, projects, and achievements. What challenges have you overcome? What projects have you led? Quantify your achievements whenever possible. Numbers and specific outcomes add weight to your accomplishments.

3. Assess Your Unique Selling Points: What sets you apart from others in your field? It could be a unique combination of skills, a successful project, or even your ability to adapt quickly to new technologies. Identify these unique selling points; they are your secret weapons in negotiations.

4. Seek Feedback: Reach out to colleagues, supervisors, or mentors for feedback. They can provide valuable insights into your strengths and areas where you excel. Sometimes, others see qualities in us that we might overlook.

5. Compare with Industry Standards: Compare your skills and experiences with industry standards. How do your qualifications stack up against the requirements for similar roles in the market? Identify any gaps and work on bridging them through additional training or certifications.

Crafting Your Value Proposition:
Once you have a clear understanding of your skills and value, craft a compelling value proposition. This is a concise statement that encapsulates what you bring to the table. It should highlight your unique skills, experiences, and achievements. Your value proposition becomes the backbone of your negotiation pitch, demonstrating to employers why you are worth the salary you're seeking.

Remember, your value is not just about what you do; it's about how effectively you do it and the impact you create. Assessing your value equips you with the self-assurance needed to negotiate confidently and persuasively. So, invest the time to introspect, recognize your strengths, and get ready to showcase your value in the competitive landscape of software engineering. Your skills are your currency, make sure you know their true worth.

Identifying Your Ideal Salary Range

One of the pivotal steps in preparing for a successful salary negotiation is determining your ideal salary range. This section is all about finding that sweet spot—a figure that reflects your worth, aligns with industry standards and meets your financial goals. Identifying your ideal salary range provides you with a clear target during negotiations, helping you navigate the conversation with confidence and precision.

Why Identifying Your Ideal Salary Range is Crucial:

1. Clarity and Focus: Pinpointing your ideal salary range provides clarity. It narrows down the vast spectrum of possible salaries to a specific, manageable range, allowing you to focus your negotiation strategy effectively.

2. Realistic Expectations: Setting a realistic salary range ensures that your expectations are grounded. It prevents you from aiming too high, which could jeopardize the negotiation, or setting the bar too low, undervaluing your skills and experience.

3. Negotiation Leverage: Armed with a well-researched ideal salary range, you enter negotiations with a strong position. You can confidently articulate your expectations and provide valid reasons for why your desired salary falls within this range.

Steps to Identify Your Ideal Salary Range:

1. Evaluate Your Financial Needs: Consider your living expenses, debts, savings goals, and other financial commitments. Determine the minimum salary you require to maintain your desired lifestyle comfortably.

2. Research Industry Standards: Refer back to the salary benchmarks you researched earlier. Identify the average salary range for professionals with your skills and experience level in your location. This serves as a benchmark to ensure your expectations align with industry norms.

3. Factor in Your Experience and Expertise: If you possess specialized skills, certifications, or significant years of experience, these factors can justify a higher salary. Take them into account when defining the upper limit of your ideal salary range.

4. Consider Benefits and Perks: Remember that salary negotiation isn't just about the base pay. Consider the value of benefits such as health insurance, retirement plans, bonuses, and other perks. These can influence your overall compensation package and widen your acceptable salary range.

5. Account for Career Growth: Think long-term. Factor in potential career growth and how your salary might evolve as you gain more experience, take on additional responsibilities, or acquire new skills. Your ideal salary range should be flexible enough to accommodate future advancements in your career.

6. Practice Flexibility: While having a specific range in mind is crucial, be open to slight adjustments based on the overall compensation package and the opportunities for growth within the company. Flexibility can demonstrate your willingness to work collaboratively with the employer.

Refining Your Ideal Salary Range:
After considering these factors, you'll have a defined salary range that aligns with your financial needs, industry standards, and personal aspirations. This range becomes your anchor during negotiations. It empowers you to confidently communicate your expectations and engage in a constructive dialogue with potential employers.

Remember, identifying your ideal salary range is not about underselling yourself or aiming for the highest number possible; it's about finding a balance that reflects your value while being fair and competitive within the industry. With a clear salary range in mind, you're well-prepared to enter negotiations, advocate for your worth, and secure a compensation package that recognizes your skills and contributions effectively.

Gathering Supporting Documentation

In the intricate dance of salary negotiations, facts and figures can be your best friends. Gathering supporting documentation is akin to assembling your arsenal, a collection of evidence that substantiates your worth and strengthens your negotiating position. This section explores the importance of documentation, what to gather, and how to present it effectively to leave a lasting impression during your negotiation.

Why Gathering Supporting Documentation is Essential:

1. Credibility: Concrete data lends credibility to your claims. When you can back up your statements with facts, employers are more likely to take your arguments seriously and view you as a knowledgeable, well-prepared candidate.

2. Confidence Booster: Having well-researched data at your fingertips boosts your confidence. You enter negotiations with assurance, knowing you have solid evidence to support your salary expectations, which can significantly impact the outcome of the conversation.

3. Professionalism: Presenting supporting documentation showcases your professionalism and attention to detail. It demonstrates that you approach negotiations methodically and are serious about your expectations, leaving a positive impression on potential employers.

Types of Supporting Documentation to Gather:

1. Market Research: Collate data from reliable sources like industry reports, salary surveys, and online platforms. Highlight the average salaries for professionals with similar qualifications and experience in your geographic area. This information serves as a benchmark for your negotiations.

2. Your Achievements: Prepare a list of your accomplishments, both big and small. Include details about projects you've led, problems you've solved, and any awards or recognitions received. Quantify your achievements whenever possible, emphasizing the value you brought to your previous roles.

3. Certifications and Qualifications: If you have relevant certifications or advanced degrees, gather copies of these documents. Highlight how these qualifications enhance your skills and contribute to your suitability for the position.

4. Letters of Recommendation: Collect letters of recommendation from previous employers, colleagues, or clients. Positive testimonials from people you've worked with can reinforce your professional reputation and demonstrate your impact in previous roles.

5. Performance Reviews: If applicable, include excerpts from your performance reviews that highlight your strengths, achievements, and contributions to the company. Positive feedback from supervisors can carry significant weight during negotiations.

Presenting Your Documentation Effectively:

1. Organize Your Materials: Arrange your documentation logically, categorizing it into sections such as market research, achievements, certifications, and testimonials. This makes it easy to access specific information during the negotiation conversation.

2. Create a Visual Presentation: Consider creating a visual presentation summarizing your key points. Visual aids, such as charts and graphs, can help convey complex information in an easily digestible format, leaving a lasting impression on your audience.

3. Practice Articulating Your Points: Familiarize yourself with the content of your documentation.

Practice articulating your achievements and qualifications confidently. Be prepared to discuss how your skills align with the company's needs and how your contributions can positively impact their goals.

4. Be Open to Discussion: While your documentation provides a strong foundation, be open to discussing and elaborating on the points you present. Engage in a constructive conversation, addressing any questions or concerns the employer might have regarding your supporting materials.

Gathering supporting documentation is not just about arming yourself with data; it's about presenting a compelling narrative of your skills, achievements, and value to the potential employer. With a well-prepared arsenal of facts and figures, you'll be equipped to negotiate with confidence, leaving a lasting impression and increasing your chances of securing the salary you deserve.

Chapter 2

Building Your Negotiation Toolkit

Mastering the Art of Effective Communication

Welcome to the heart of your salary negotiation journey, mastering the art of effective communication. In this chapter, we will explore the power of words, body language, and active listening. Effective communication is not just about what you say; it's about how you say it when you say it, and even what you don't say. By honing your communication skills, you'll transform simple conversations into persuasive negotiations.

The Role of Effective Communication in Salary Negotiations:

Effective communication is the cornerstone of successful negotiations. It's not just a tool; it's your secret weapon. Here's why it matters:

1. Building Rapport: Engaging in open, honest, and respectful communication helps build rapport with your potential employer. A positive rapport sets the stage for constructive negotiations and fosters a sense of mutual understanding.

2. Clarifying Expectations: Clear communication ensures that both parties understand each other's expectations. It helps eliminate misunderstandings and creates a shared understanding of what is being negotiated, be it salary, benefits, or job responsibilities.

3. Overcoming Objections: Through effective communication, you can address concerns and objections raised by the employer. Listening actively allows you to identify these concerns and respond thoughtfully, turning potential roadblocks into opportunities for resolution.

4. Confidence and Assertiveness: Effective communication breeds confidence. When you can articulate your points clearly and assertively, you project confidence in your abilities and the value you bring to the table.

Key Components of Effective Communication:

1. Active Listening: The foundation of effective communication lies in active listening. Pay attention to not only the words being said but also the tone, emotions, and underlying messages. By listening actively, you demonstrate respect and empathy, creating a conducive environment for negotiations.

2. Clarity and Conciseness: Be clear and concise in your communication. Avoid jargon and technical terms that the other party might not understand. Clearly state your points and provide specific examples to illustrate your achievements and qualifications.

3. Empathy and Understanding: Put yourself in the shoes of the other party. Understand their perspective, concerns, and needs. Empathetic communication shows that you value their viewpoint, fostering a collaborative atmosphere.

4. Confidence and Body Language: Confidence is not just about what you say; it's also about how you say it. Maintain eye contact, use confident body language, and speak with a steady tone. Confident body language exudes assurance and conviction.

5. Negotiation Scripts: Prepare well-thought-out negotiation scripts in advance. Anticipate potential questions and objections and craft persuasive responses. Having a script as a reference ensures you stay on track and convey your points effectively.

Practice and Preparation:

1. Role-Playing Exercises: Engage in role-playing exercises with a friend or mentor. Practice different negotiation scenarios, allowing you to refine your communication skills and responses to various situations.

2. Feedback and Iteration: Seek feedback from trusted colleagues or mentors. They can provide valuable insights into your communication style, helping you identify areas for improvement. Iterate and refine your communication approach based on the feedback received.

3. Mindful Communication: Be mindful of your words and tone. Avoid confrontational language and focus on collaborative, solution-oriented communication. Mindful communication fosters a positive atmosphere, conducive to successful negotiations.

Mastering the art of effective communication is not just a negotiation skill, it's a life skill. The ability to communicate, confidently, and empathetically can open doors, strengthen relationships, and, most importantly, help you secure the salary and opportunities you deserve.

Crafting a Compelling Personal Pitch

Imagine stepping into a salary negotiation armed with a captivating story, one that not only showcases your skills and achievements but also leaves a lasting impression on your potential employer. Crafting a compelling personal pitch is your opportunity to do just that. In this section, we'll explore the art of storytelling and how to tailor your narrative to emphasize your unique value proposition.

Why a Personal Pitch Matters:
Your pitch is more than just an introduction; it's a strategic tool that can set the tone for your entire negotiation. Here's why it matters:

1. Memorability: A well-crafted personal pitch is memorable. It leaves a strong impression on the listener, making you stand out among other candidates. A memorable pitch is more likely to be remembered and discussed during the decision-making process.

2. Clarity: Your pitch should convey your skills, experiences, and goals clearly and succinctly. A clear and concise pitch ensures that your potential employer understands your value proposition, making it easier for them to consider you for the position.

3. Engagement: A compelling personal pitch captivates the listener's attention. It engages them on a personal level, making them more receptive to your message. Engaged listeners are more likely to respond positively to your negotiation points.

Crafting Your Pitch:

1. Start with a Hook: Begin your pitch with a strong opening that grabs attention. This could be a personal anecdote, a surprising fact, or a thought-provoking question related to your industry or achievements.

2. Highlight Your Achievements: Focus on your key accomplishments and experiences. Use quantifiable data to illustrate your impact. Numbers and specific outcomes make your achievements more tangible and impressive.

3. Emphasize Your Unique Selling Points: What sets you apart from other candidates? Whether it's a unique skill, a specific project, or your ability to solve complex problems, emphasize these unique selling points in your pitch.

4. Relate to the Company: Connect your skills and experiences to the needs of the company. Research the organization thoroughly and tailor your pitch to demonstrate how you can contribute to their specific goals and challenges.

5. Inject Passion and Enthusiasm: Show genuine passion for your work and the industry. Enthusiasm is contagious and can leave a lasting impression. Employers are more likely to be enthusiastic about hiring someone genuinely excited about the role.

6. Practice and Refine: Practice your pitch multiple times. Rehearse in front of a mirror, with a friend, or record yourself. Pay attention to your tone, pacing, and body language. Refine your pitch based on feedback to make it more compelling.

Adapting Your Pitch for Different Situations:
Tailor your pitch based on the context of the negotiation. Whether you're in a formal interview, a networking event, or a casual conversation, adapt your pitch to suit the situation. A versatile pitch allows you to make a strong impression in various scenarios.

Closing Your Pitch with Confidence:
End your pitch with a confident closing statement. Express your enthusiasm for the opportunity, thank the listener for their time, and express your eagerness to discuss how you can contribute further. A confident closing leaves a positive, lasting impression.

Crafting a compelling personal pitch is an art that combines your unique story with the needs of the employer. It's your chance to showcase your skills, achievements, and passion in a way that resonates with your potential employer. With a captivating personal pitch, you'll not only leave a lasting impression but also set the stage for successful salary negotiations. So, invest time and effort in perfecting your pitch—it might just be the key to unlocking the salary and career opportunities you desire.

Strategies for Negotiation Success

Negotiating your salary isn't a battle; it's a strategic conversation. In this section, we will explore a set of effective strategies designed to help you navigate the negotiation process with finesse and confidence. These strategies are your secret weapons, enabling you to steer the conversation in your favor and secure the compensation you deserve.

1. Knowledge is Power:

The foundation of any successful negotiation is knowledge. Research extensively about the company, its industry, and standard salary ranges for your role. Understand the company's financial health, recent successes, and challenges. The more you know, the better equipped you are to make a compelling case for your worth.

2. Aim High (Within Reason):

Set your initial salary request slightly higher than your ideal range. This provides room for negotiation and allows you to make concessions without compromising your desired salary. However, be realistic; your initial request should still fall within industry standards and align with your qualifications.

3. Focus on the Value You Bring:

During the negotiation, shift the focus from what you need to what you bring to the table. Emphasize your skills, experiences, and achievements that align with the company's objectives. Discuss how your contributions can solve their challenges, improve processes, or drive revenue. Demonstrating your value strengthens your position.

4. Practice the Pause:

Silence can be a powerful negotiating tool. After stating your salary expectations or counteroffer, practice the pause. Give the other party time to respond. Silence can create discomfort, prompting the other party to make concessions or offer additional benefits. Stay composed and let the pause work to your advantage.

5. Be Confident, Not Aggressive:

Confidence is key, but it should never spill over into aggression. Maintain a respectful and professional tone throughout the negotiation. Firmly state your points, but avoid sounding confrontational. A confident, yet approachable demeanor fosters a positive atmosphere and encourages collaborative discussions.

6. Master the Art of Compromise:

Understand that negotiations often involve give and take. Be open to compromise, especially on non-salary aspects such as benefits, work hours, or professional development opportunities. Prioritize your needs but be willing to make concessions that demonstrate flexibility and a willingness to collaborate.

7. Practice Active Listening:
Effective negotiation is a two-way street. Listen actively to the other party's concerns, questions, and objections. Acknowledge their points and respond thoughtfully. Addressing their concerns demonstrates empathy and shows that you value their perspective, paving the way for constructive dialogue.

8. Have a Backup Plan:
Prepare for different scenarios. What will you do if the employer can't meet your salary expectations? Having a backup plan, such as additional benefits or performance-based bonuses, allows you to remain flexible while ensuring you achieve a favorable outcome.

9. Know When to Walk Away:
While negotiations are essential, it's equally crucial to recognize when an offer does not align with your value. If the employer consistently fails to meet your reasonable expectations, it might be a sign that the company undervalues its employees. In such cases, be prepared to walk away and explore opportunities where your skills are truly appreciated.

10. *Follow Up Professionally:*

After reaching an agreement, follow up with a professional email expressing gratitude for the offer and confirming the details discussed. A prompt and polite follow-up demonstrates your professionalism and leaves a positive impression, setting the stage for a successful transition into your new role.

By implementing these strategies, you'll approach negotiations not as a daunting challenge, but as an opportunity to showcase your value and secure a compensation package that reflects your skills and contributions. Remember, negotiation is a skill that improves with practice and experience. With each negotiation, you'll refine your approach, becoming more adept at articulating your worth and achieving the outcomes you desire. So, step into the negotiation room with confidence, armed with these strategies, and pave the way for your success.

Overcoming Common Salary Negotiation Challenges

Navigating a salary negotiation is no walk in the park; challenges and obstacles are bound to arise. In this section, we'll discuss some of the most common challenges you might face during salary negotiations and provide strategies to overcome them with confidence.

1. The Fear of Rejection:

Challenge: Many individuals fear rejection during salary negotiations. They worry that by asking for more, they might lose the job offer altogether.

Strategy: Remember that negotiation is a standard part of the hiring process. Employers anticipate candidates negotiating, and it's rare for a negotiation to lead to a rescinded job offer. Focus on the potential gains from negotiation and the confidence it conveys rather than the fear of rejection.

2. Navigating Counteroffers:

Challenge: Handling counteroffers can be tricky. You've made your initial request, and the employer has countered with an offer below your expectations. How do you respond effectively?

Strategy: Remain open to counteroffers, and treat them as opportunities for continued negotiation. Express gratitude for the counteroffer and politely restate your points, highlighting your value and justifying your initial request. Be prepared to make measured concessions, but avoid compromising too quickly.

3. Balancing Confidence and Humility:

Challenge: Striking the right balance between confidence and humility can be challenging. You want to assert your value without coming across as arrogant.

Strategy: Confidence is essential, but it should be combined with humility and professionalism. Focus on your skills and achievements rather than boasting. Demonstrate your enthusiasm for the role and your willingness to collaborate, which creates a positive impression.

4. Dealing with Non-Negotiable Offers:

Challenge: Some employers may present non-negotiable offers, particularly in highly structured organizations or for entry-level positions.

Strategy: If faced with a non-negotiable offer, consider other aspects of the job such as benefits, work-life balance, and growth opportunities. Negotiate for improvements in these areas if the base salary is not flexible. If the offer truly does not meet your needs, you may need to consider whether the job is the right fit for you.

5. Emotional Responses:

Challenge: Negotiations can be emotionally charged. You might feel anxiety, frustration, or even anger during the process, especially when the outcome is critical.

Strategy: Recognize that emotions are normal but should be managed during negotiations. Take deep breaths, pause, and remind yourself of your prepared points. Focus on the facts and remain composed. Emotional control enables more effective communication.

6. Handling Multiple Offers:

Challenge: If you have multiple job offers on the table, it can be challenging to navigate negotiations effectively without inadvertently pitting employers against each other.

Strategy: Be transparent but professional. Communicate that you have multiple offers and express your preference for the current position. Use this as an opportunity to inquire if the current employer can improve their offer. Maintain respect for all parties involved, even if you end up declining an offer.

7. Patience and Persistence:

Challenge: Negotiations can be time-consuming and require patience. It's common to go back and forth with the employer before reaching an agreement.

Strategy: Be patient and persistent. Understand that negotiations may take time, and multiple rounds of discussion may be needed. Stick to your research and value proposition, and keep the lines of communication open.

By recognizing and preparing for these common salary negotiation challenges, you can approach negotiations with greater confidence and resilience. Remember that negotiation is a dynamic process, and your ability to adapt and overcome obstacles is a valuable skill that you'll continue to refine over time. Stay focused on your goals, maintain professionalism, and be persistent in pursuing the compensation and opportunities you deserve.

Chapter 3

The Negotiation Process

Initiating the Salary Negotiation

Congratulations! You've landed the job offer, and now it's time to embark on the salary negotiation journey. Initiating the salary negotiation can feel like stepping onto a tightrope, but with the right approach, you can navigate this crucial phase with confidence and finesse. In this section, we'll explore the art of initiating the negotiation process and setting the stage for a successful conversation.

1. Timing Is Key:
Strategy: Choose an appropriate time to initiate the negotiation. Ideally, wait until you receive a formal job offer in writing. Once you have the offer in hand, express your gratitude for the opportunity and indicate your eagerness to discuss the details, including compensation. Avoid rushing the process; patience demonstrates professionalism.

2. Express Enthusiasm:

Strategy: Begin the conversation on a positive note. Express your genuine enthusiasm for the role and the company. Emphasize your excitement about contributing to their success. Positive energy sets a collaborative tone and fosters a more receptive atmosphere for negotiation.

3. Prepare Your Talking Points:

Strategy: Prepare a list of key talking points to discuss during the negotiation. Highlight your skills, qualifications, and relevant achievements. Reference industry benchmarks and market research to support your request. Practice articulating these points clearly and confidently to make a compelling case.

4. Be Clear and Confident:

Strategy: Clearly state your request for a higher salary with confidence. Use assertive language, maintaining a professional and respectful tone. Be specific about your expectations and avoid vague statements. Clarity and confidence enhance your credibility and increase the likelihood of a positive response.

5. Acknowledge Their Offer:

Strategy: Acknowledge the initial offer graciously, even if it falls below your expectations. Express appreciation for the opportunity and the effort put into the offer. By acknowledging their offer respectfully, you demonstrate professionalism and create a foundation for a constructive conversation.

6. Emphasize Your Value Proposition:
Strategy: Take the opportunity to reiterate your value proposition. Discuss your relevant skills, experiences, and achievements. Explain how your contributions align with the company's goals and how investing in your talents will benefit their organization. Connecting your request to your potential impact strengthens your negotiation stance.

7. Practice Active Listening:
Strategy: Actively listen to the employer's response. Pay attention to their concerns, questions, and any objections raised. Acknowledge their points, and respond thoughtfully. Active listening demonstrates your respect for their perspective and opens the door for a more collaborative discussion.

8. Be Prepared for Questions:
Strategy: Anticipate questions the employer might ask during the negotiation. Common questions include inquiries about your salary expectations, reasons for the request, and how you arrived at your figure. Prepare concise and compelling answers to these questions, reinforcing the validity of your request.

9. Be Open to Discussion:

Strategy: Be open to discussing not only the base salary but also other aspects of the compensation package, such as benefits, bonuses, or additional perks. A flexible approach demonstrates your willingness to find mutually beneficial solutions and showcases your adaptability.

10. Express Gratitude Regardless of the Outcome:

Strategy: Regardless of the negotiation's outcome, express gratitude for the employer's time and consideration. If an agreement is reached, convey your appreciation for their flexibility. If the negotiation does not meet your expectations, remain professional and express gratitude for the opportunity, leaving the door open for future engagements.

Initiating the salary negotiation sets the tone for the entire conversation. By approaching this phase with preparation, confidence, and respect, you establish a strong foundation for a collaborative discussion. Remember, negotiation is a dialogue, not a confrontation. With a well-prepared mindset and strategic approach, you increase your chances of securing a compensation package that reflects your true worth and contributions.

Navigating Initial Offers and Counteroffers

Negotiating initial offers and counteroffers is a delicate dance, requiring strategic finesse and effective communication. In this section, we'll delve into the art of navigating the intricacies of both initial offers and subsequent counteroffers, equipping you with the skills to handle these critical stages of negotiation successfully.

1. Evaluating the Initial Offer:
Strategy: Carefully review the initial offer, considering not only the base salary but also the entire compensation package. Assess benefits, bonuses, retirement plans, and other perks offered. Compare the offer to industry standards and your research to determine if it meets your expectations and financial needs.

2. Express Appreciation:
Strategy: Express gratitude for the initial offer, regardless of whether it aligns with your expectations. Demonstrating appreciation sets a positive tone for the negotiation. Acknowledge the effort put into the offer, reinforcing your interest in the position.

3. Responding to an Initial Offer:
Strategy: If the initial offer falls below your expectations, respond professionally and assertively.

Politely express your gratitude and reiterate your enthusiasm for the role. Clearly state your counteroffer, supported by market research and your value proposition. Be specific about the aspects you wish to negotiate, such as salary, benefits, or bonuses.

4. Handling Counteroffers:
Strategy: When presented with a counteroffer, carefully evaluate it. Consider both the financial aspects and any additional perks or benefits offered. If the counteroffer is acceptable, express your appreciation and acceptance clearly. If it still falls short, respond respectfully, restate your points, and negotiate further if necessary. Avoid accepting an offer immediately; take the time to evaluate it thoroughly.

5. Demonstrating Flexibility:
Strategy: While it's essential to stand firm on your priorities, demonstrate flexibility where possible. Be open to compromises, especially in non-salary aspects of the offer. A willingness to collaborate and find mutually beneficial solutions can foster a positive negotiating atmosphere.

6. Handling Multiple Offers:
Strategy: If you're juggling multiple job offers, handle the situation with transparency and professionalism. Inform all parties involved about the existence of other

offers without divulging specific details. Express your preference for the current position and inquire if there is room for improvement in the offer. Use multiple offers as an opportunity to negotiate more effectively.

7. Managing Impersonal Negotiations:

Strategy: In some cases, negotiations may occur through email or other written communication, lacking face-to-face interaction. In such situations, be clear, concise, and polite in your written responses. Clearly articulate your points, supported by data and evidence, to make a persuasive case.

8. Knowing When to Conclude Negotiations:

Strategy: Negotiations should continue until both parties reach an agreement or it becomes evident that further discussions are unlikely to yield positive results. If the employer is unable or unwilling to meet your reasonable expectations, gracefully conclude the negotiations. Express gratitude for the opportunity and remain professional. Leave the door open for future engagements, as relationships are valuable in the professional world.

Navigating initial offers and counteroffers requires a blend of confidence, patience, and adaptability. By approaching these stages of negotiation with professionalism, gratitude, and a clear understanding of your value, you position yourself as a strong, capable candidate. Remember, negotiation is a dialogue, and the key to success lies in effective communication and a collaborative spirit. With these strategies in your toolkit, you're well-prepared to navigate the complexities of initial offers and counteroffers, securing a compensation package that aligns with your worth and aspirations.

Handling Salary Negotiations During Job Interviews

Navigating salary discussions during job interviews can be both exciting and challenging. This section will guide you through the intricacies of discussing compensation during interviews, providing you with the strategies to handle these conversations confidently and professionally.

1. Research Thoroughly:

Strategy: Conduct extensive research on the company, industry standards, and the specific role you're interviewing for. Understand the typical salary range for similar positions in the company's location and industry. Armed with this information, you can approach the negotiation conversation with confidence.

2. Timing Is Crucial:

Strategy: Ideally, avoid discussing salary in the early stages of the interview process. Focus on showcasing your skills, experience, and enthusiasm for the role first. If the interviewer brings up the topic, handle it gracefully. If possible, defer the discussion until you have a comprehensive understanding of the job requirements and the employer's expectations.

3. Be Prepared to Deflect:

Strategy: If asked about your salary expectations before you are ready, deflect the question tactfully. Politely express your enthusiasm for the role and your focus on finding the right fit. Offer a general range based on your research and emphasize your willingness to discuss compensation further once you have a deeper understanding of the position.

4. Shift the Focus to Value:

Strategy: During the interview, shift the conversation toward the value you bring to the organization. Discuss your skills, accomplishments, and how your expertise aligns with the company's goals. By emphasizing your value, you create a strong foundation for negotiating a competitive salary later in the process.

5. Practice Active Listening:

Strategy: Pay close attention to any hints or signals the interviewer gives about the salary range or benefits. Listen actively to their questions and concerns. Understanding their perspective allows you to tailor your responses effectively and address their specific needs during the negotiation phase.

6. Be Transparent and Honest:

Strategy: Be transparent about your salary history and expectations when the topic arises. Honesty builds trust, and it's essential for a successful working relationship. If you're asked about your current salary, provide accurate information. When discussing your expectations, be clear, realistic, and open to negotiation.

7. Express Flexibility:
Strategy: Demonstrate flexibility in your negotiation approach. While you should have a clear understanding of your worth, be open to discussing different aspects of the compensation package, such as benefits, bonuses, or professional development opportunities. Express your willingness to collaborate and find mutually beneficial solutions.

8. Practice, Prepare, and Role-Play:
Strategy: Practice your responses to common salary-related questions. Prepare concise yet compelling answers that highlight your value and address potential concerns. Consider role-playing with a friend or mentor to simulate interview scenarios. Practicing your responses boosts your confidence and helps you handle unexpected questions more effectively.

Handling salary negotiations during job interviews requires a delicate balance of confidence, professionalism, and adaptability. By conducting thorough research, focusing on your values, and being transparent yet flexible, you position yourself as a candidate who understands your worth and is ready to engage in a constructive negotiation dialogue. With these strategies in place, you'll be well-equipped to navigate salary discussions during job interviews successfully, ensuring that your compensation aligns with your skills and contributions.

Negotiating Benefits and Perks

Negotiating benefits and perks is a vital component of the overall compensation package. Beyond the base salary, these additional offerings can significantly impact your work-life balance and job satisfaction. This section explores effective strategies to negotiate benefits and perks, ensuring you secure a comprehensive and appealing compensation package.

1. Understand the Full Benefits Package:
Strategy: Before entering negotiations, thoroughly understand the benefits offered by the company. This includes health insurance, retirement plans, paid time off, bonuses, stock options, professional development opportunities, and other perks like remote work flexibility or gym memberships. A comprehensive understanding enables you to negotiate from an informed position.

2. Prioritize Your Needs:
Strategy: Identify the benefits and perks that matter most to you. Whether it's comprehensive healthcare coverage, a flexible work schedule, or opportunities for skill development, prioritize your needs. Focus your negotiation efforts on areas that align with your personal and professional goals.

3. Quantify the Value:

Strategy: When negotiating benefits, quantify their value. For example, if the company offers education assistance, calculate the cost of the courses you plan to take. If negotiating remote work options, emphasize how it enhances your productivity and work-life balance. Quantifying the benefits demonstrates their tangible value to you and the company.

4. Link Benefits to Performance:

Strategy: Showcase how certain benefits can enhance your performance and contribute to the company's success. For instance, if you're negotiating professional development opportunities, explain how additional training will improve your skills and allow you to take on more responsibilities. Linking benefits to your performance emphasizes their relevance and value in a professional context.

5. Highlight Company Culture:

Strategy: Emphasize how certain perks align with the company's culture and your motivation to be a part of it. For instance, if the company values work-life balance, negotiating for additional vacation days or remote work options aligns with the organization's ethos. Demonstrating your alignment with the company culture strengthens your negotiation position.

6. Be Open to Creativity:

Strategy: Think creatively about benefits and perks. Consider options beyond the standard offerings. Negotiate for unique benefits tailored to your needs, such as a stipend for professional memberships, wellness programs, or opportunities for sabbaticals. Creativity in negotiation showcases your adaptability and innovative thinking.

7. Leverage Multiple Offers:

Strategy: If you have multiple job offers, leverage them strategically. Use the benefits offered by one company as leverage to negotiate with another. Be respectful and professional in your approach, emphasizing your preference for the current position but expressing the desire for a competitive benefits package.

8. Seek Professional Advice:

Strategy: If the benefits package is complex or you're uncertain about certain aspects, consider seeking advice from a professional, such as a financial advisor or HR consultant. They can provide valuable insights and help you make informed decisions about negotiating benefits and perks.

9. Read the Fine Print:

Strategy: Pay close attention to the terms and conditions associated with the benefits and perks offered.

Understand any limitations or restrictions, especially concerning benefits like stock options or retirement plans. Being aware of the fine print ensures you make well-informed decisions during negotiations.

10. Express Gratitude and Professionalism:
Strategy: Regardless of the outcome, express gratitude for the company's willingness to discuss benefits and perks. Maintain professionalism throughout the negotiation process, even if certain requests cannot be accommodated. A positive, respectful attitude leaves a lasting impression and fosters a constructive working relationship.

Negotiating benefits and perks is an opportunity to tailor your compensation package to your unique needs and preferences. By understanding the value, linking benefits to your performance, and approaching negotiations creatively, you can secure a benefits package that enhances your overall job satisfaction and well-being. Remember, effective negotiation is not just about what you receive but also about building positive, collaborative relationships with your employer.

Chapter 4

Sealing the Deal

Finalizing the Offer

Congratulations! You've navigated the intricate maze of negotiations and are on the verge of sealing the deal. In this section, we'll explore the essential steps to finalize the offer, ensuring a smooth transition from negotiations to acceptance and setting the stage for a successful start to your new position.

1. Clarify the Offer in Detail:
Strategy: Request a detailed written offer that outlines all aspects of your compensation package, including base salary, bonuses, benefits, perks, vacation days, and any other allowances. Review this document meticulously to ensure it aligns with the negotiated terms. If there are discrepancies, address them promptly to avoid misunderstandings later.

2. Seek Legal and Financial Advice (if necessary):
Strategy: If your compensation package includes complex elements such as stock options, deferred compensation, or intricate bonuses, consider consulting a

financial advisor or legal expert. Their insights can help you understand the terms fully and make informed decisions, ensuring you are protected and maximizing your financial benefits.

3. Express Appreciation and Enthusiasm:

Strategy: Respond to the formal offer with a professional and appreciative tone. Express your gratitude for the opportunity and enthusiasm for joining the company. A well-crafted response reinforces your interest in the position and sets a positive tone for your future interactions.

4. Negotiate Any Outstanding Points:

Strategy: If there are lingering issues or details that need further clarification, address them promptly and professionally. It's crucial to resolve any outstanding points before formally accepting the offer. Be clear, concise, and respectful in your communication, focusing on finding mutually beneficial solutions.

5. Confirm the Start Date and Onboarding Process:

Strategy: Clarify your start date and the onboarding process with the company. Understand the schedule for orientation, training, and any initial meetings. Being well-informed about your first days on the job helps you prepare effectively and ensures a smooth transition into your new role.

6. Review Company Policies and Culture:
Strategy: Familiarize yourself with the company's policies, culture, and expectations. Understand the dress code, working hours, communication protocols, and any other guidelines. Aligning yourself with the company's ethos enhances your ability to integrate seamlessly into the organizational environment.

7. Prepare for Your First Day:
Strategy: Plan for your first day by organizing your commute, selecting appropriate attire, and gathering any necessary documents or materials. Prepare questions you might have for your supervisor or HR representative. Being proactive and well-prepared demonstrates your professionalism and enthusiasm for the new role.

8. Follow Up with Gratitude:
Strategy: After finalizing the offer and preparing for your new position, follow up with a final expression of gratitude. Send a thank-you email to your main contact person, reiterating your excitement for the opportunity and appreciation for their support throughout the process. A thoughtful follow-up message reinforces your professionalism and leaves a positive impression.

9. Stay Professional and Positive:

Strategy: Maintain a positive and professional attitude during the entire process. Even if there are challenges or uncertainties, approach them with grace and optimism. A positive mindset reflects your resilience and adaptability, essential qualities in any professional setting.

10. Prepare to Excel:

Strategy: Use the time before your start date to prepare mentally and emotionally for your new role. Reflect on your goals, review your skills and accomplishments, and visualize your success in the position. Arriving with confidence and a positive mindset positions you for a successful and fulfilling career journey.

Sealing the deal and finalizing the offer marks the culmination of your negotiation efforts. By approaching this phase with attention to detail, professionalism, and gratitude, you set the stage for a positive and productive relationship with your new employer. Remember, the negotiation process is not just about securing a job; it's about laying the foundation for a successful and rewarding career. With your efforts and thoughtful approach, you're well on your way to achieving your professional aspirations.

The Importance of Written Agreements

In the realm of professional negotiations, the written agreement stands as a cornerstone, providing a clear, documented record of the terms and conditions agreed upon by both parties. In this section, we'll explore the crucial importance of written agreements in the context of salary negotiations and employment contracts.

1. Clarity and Avoiding Misunderstandings:

Strategy: A written agreement serves as a definitive record of the negotiated terms. It leaves no room for ambiguity or misunderstandings that verbal agreements might entail. Having every detail clearly stated minimizes the possibility of miscommunication, ensuring that both parties are on the same page regarding the terms of employment.

2. Legal Protection:

Strategy: A written agreement provides legal protection for both the employer and the employee. It outlines the rights and responsibilities of each party, reducing the risk of disputes and legal complications in the future. If any disagreements arise, the written agreement serves as a legally binding document that can be referenced to resolve conflicts.

3. Reference Point for Both Parties:

Strategy: The written agreement acts as a reference point throughout the employment period. It serves as a guide for both the employer and the employee, reminding them of the agreed-upon terms regarding salary, benefits, job responsibilities, and any other relevant details. This reference ensures that everyone adheres to the terms, fostering a professional and compliant work environment.

4. Building Trust and Credibility:

Strategy: Providing a written agreement demonstrates professionalism, transparency, and integrity. Employers who present a comprehensive, well-structured written agreement show their commitment to fair employment practices. For employees, signing a written agreement signifies trust in the employer and confidence in the employment relationship. This mutual trust lays the foundation for a positive and productive work environment.

5. Facilitating Future Planning:

Strategy: Having a written agreement in place facilitates future planning for both the employer and the employee. It provides a clear understanding of the employment terms, allowing employees to plan their careers and personal lives with certainty. Employers can also make informed decisions based on the agreed-upon terms, ensuring smooth business operations.

6. Ensuring Compliance with Regulations:
Strategy: Written agreements help ensure compliance with local, regional, and national employment regulations. By documenting the terms and conditions in alignment with legal requirements, employers mitigate the risk of legal issues and financial penalties. For employees, a written agreement assures that their rights are protected by labor laws.

7. Clarifying Confidentiality and Non-Compete Clauses:
Strategy: In addition to salary and job responsibilities, written agreements often include clauses related to confidentiality and non-compete agreements. These clauses are essential for protecting sensitive company information and preventing employees from working for competitors after leaving the organization. Clearly defined terms in a written agreement uphold the integrity and security of the business.

8. Navigating Changing Circumstances:
Strategy: As circumstances change, written agreements can be amended through formal processes. Having a written record simplifies the process of modifying terms, ensuring that changes are agreed upon by both parties.

This flexibility allows employers and employees to adapt to evolving needs without confusion or conflict.

In summary, a written agreement is a fundamental component of the employment relationship, providing clarity, legal protection, and a basis for mutual trust. It serves as a testament to the professionalism and commitment of both the employer and the employee. By valuing the importance of written agreements, individuals entering the workforce can establish a solid foundation for a successful, secure, and fulfilling career journey.

Accepting the Offer Gracefully

Receiving a job offer is a moment of triumph and the culmination of your efforts throughout the application and negotiation process. How you accept the offer speaks volumes about your professionalism and sets the tone for your future relationship with the employer. In this section, we'll explore the art of accepting the offer gracefully, ensuring a positive start to your new role.

1. Express Genuine Gratitude:

Strategy: Begin your acceptance with a heartfelt expression of gratitude. Thank the employer for the opportunity, emphasizing your appreciation for their confidence in your abilities. A sincere expression of thanks sets a positive tone and conveys your enthusiasm for joining the organization.

2. Confirm Your Acceptance Clearly:

Strategy: Clearly state your acceptance of the offer. Use direct language to confirm your willingness to take on the position. Being straightforward demonstrates your decisiveness and professionalism. If you have any outstanding questions or need clarification on certain points, concisely address them.

3. Reiterate Your Commitment:
Strategy: Reassure the employer of your commitment to the role and the organization. Emphasize your enthusiasm for contributing to their success and your dedication to fulfilling your responsibilities. Confidence in your abilities and eagerness to make a meaningful impact reinforce your suitability for the position.

4. Confirm Terms and Conditions:
Strategy: Confirm the terms and conditions discussed during negotiations, ensuring that both parties are on the same page. Politely request a written confirmation or employment contract that outlines the agreed-upon details, including salary, benefits, start date, and any other pertinent information. Having everything documented provides clarity and avoids misunderstandings.

5. Express Professionalism in Writing:
Strategy: Follow up your verbal acceptance with a formal written acceptance letter or email. Craft a well-written message expressing your gratitude, confirming your acceptance, and reiterating your excitement about the opportunity. Use professional language and ensure the message is free of errors. A polished communication reflects your attention to detail and professionalism.

6. Be Prompt and Responsive:

Strategy: Respond to the offer promptly. Aim to accept the offer as soon as you've made your decision, ideally within a day or two of receiving it. Prompt responsiveness demonstrates your eagerness and respect for the employer's time, leaving a positive impression.

7. Maintain a Positive and Appreciative Tone:

Strategy: Throughout your communication, maintain a positive and appreciative tone. Express your enthusiasm for working with the team, contributing to the company's goals, and learning from the experience. A positive attitude fosters a welcoming atmosphere and reinforces your dedication to making a valuable contribution.

8. Prepare for Onboarding:

Strategy: After accepting the offer, proactively prepare for your onboarding process. Complete any necessary paperwork, gather required documents, and familiarize yourself with the company's policies and procedures. Being well-prepared for your first day demonstrates your readiness to integrate seamlessly into the organization.

9. Express Appreciation Once Again:

Strategy: End your communication on a high note by expressing your gratitude once again. Thank the employer for the opportunity and convey your excitement about the journey ahead. A final expression of appreciation leaves a lasting positive impression as you prepare to embark on your new role.

Accepting a job offer gracefully is more than a formality; it's an opportunity to demonstrate your professionalism, gratitude, and enthusiasm for the position. By approaching this moment with genuine appreciation and a positive, responsive attitude, you set the stage for a strong, collaborative relationship with your new employer. Remember, the way you accept the offer not only reflects your character but also paves the way for a successful and fulfilling career within the organization.

Post-Negotiation Follow-Up and Relationship Building

Successfully concluding the negotiation process doesn't mark the end of your interactions with your employer; rather, it signifies the beginning of a professional relationship. In this section, we'll explore the importance of post-negotiation follow-up and relationship building, emphasizing the significance of fostering a positive, long-lasting connection with your new employer.

1. Send a Gracious Thank-You Note:

Strategy: After the negotiations have concluded and you've accepted the offer, send a thoughtful thank-you note to express your appreciation. Acknowledge the time and effort the employer invested in the process. A gracious thank-you note demonstrates your professionalism and gratitude, leaving a positive impression.

2. Stay Organized and Informed:

Strategy: Organize all the documents and correspondence related to your employment, including the written agreement, emails, and any other communications. Stay informed about the company's policies, procedures, and upcoming events. Being well-informed showcases your proactive approach and interest in the organization.

3. Engage in Pre-Onboarding Activities:

Strategy: Participate in pre-onboarding activities if the company offers them. Attend orientation sessions, webinars, or networking events designed for new hires. Engaging in these activities demonstrates your eagerness to integrate into the company culture and learn about your new workplace.

4. Connect on Professional Networks:

Strategy: Connect with your future colleagues and supervisors on professional networking platforms, such as LinkedIn. Personalize your connection requests with a brief, courteous message expressing your excitement about joining the team. Building professional connections in advance fosters a sense of familiarity and camaraderie.

5. Prepare Thoughtful Questions:

Strategy: Prepare thoughtful questions about your role, team, and the company culture for your future colleagues and supervisors. Asking insightful questions during your early interactions demonstrates your genuine interest in understanding your role and contributing effectively.

6. Express Appreciation in Person:

Strategy: Once you start your new position, take the opportunity to express your appreciation in person. Thank your colleagues, supervisors, and HR representatives for their support during the negotiation process and your transition into the company. Personal expressions of gratitude enhance your interpersonal relationships.

7. Seek Mentorship and Guidance:
Strategy: Identify potential mentors within the organization and proactively seek their guidance. A mentor can provide valuable insights, help you navigate the company culture, and support your professional development. Building mentor-mentee relationships strengthens your network and fosters personal growth.

8. Participate Actively:
Strategy: Actively participate in team meetings, projects, and company events. Contribute meaningfully to discussions, showcase your skills, and collaborate effectively with your colleagues. Being engaged and proactive demonstrates your commitment to your role and the organization's success.

9. Showcase Your Value:
Strategy: Continuously demonstrate your value through your work. Exceed expectations, meet deadlines, and deliver exceptional results. Your performance speaks volumes about your skills and dedication, reinforcing your position as a valuable asset to the organization.

10. Stay Open to Feedback:

Strategy: Stay open to feedback and constructive criticism. Actively seek input from your colleagues and supervisors to enhance your skills and contribute more effectively. A receptive attitude demonstrates your willingness to learn and grow within the organization.

Building a strong, positive relationship with your new employer requires ongoing effort, genuine enthusiasm, and a proactive approach. By staying engaged, expressing gratitude, seeking mentorship, and showcasing your value, you not only integrate seamlessly into the organization but also establish yourself as a valuable, respected member of the team. Remember, successful relationships are built on mutual respect, open communication, and a genuine commitment to collaboration and growth.

Chapter 5

Special Considerations

Negotiating Salary in Different Work Environments (Startups, Corporations, Remote Work)

Negotiating salary can vary significantly based on the work environment you're in. Whether you're dealing with the dynamic atmosphere of a startup, the structured environment of a corporation, or the flexibility of remote work, understanding the unique nuances of each setting is crucial for successful negotiations. In this section, we'll explore the special considerations involved in negotiating salary in startups, corporations, and remote work scenarios.

1. Negotiating Salary in Startups:
Strategy: Startups often operate in a fast-paced, high-risk environment where resources are limited. When negotiating salary in a startup, consider the company's financial stability and growth potential. While startups might offer lower initial salaries, they often compensate with equity, promising a share in the

company's success. Evaluate the equity offer carefully, considering its potential value in the future. Additionally, emphasize your adaptability, willingness to take on multiple roles, and entrepreneurial spirit, as startups value employees who can wear multiple hats and contribute to various aspects of the business.

2. Negotiating Salary in Corporations:

Strategy: Negotiating salary in corporations involves navigating structured hierarchies and established salary bands. Research the company's salary structure and industry standards to determine an appropriate salary range for your role. Focus on showcasing your specific skills, experiences, and achievements that align with the corporation's objectives. Emphasize how your contributions can add value to the company, making you a worthwhile investment. Be prepared to discuss not only the base salary but also bonuses, benefits, and opportunities for career advancement within the corporation.

3. Negotiating Salary for Remote Work:

Strategy: Remote work offers flexibility but may come with its own set of challenges in negotiations. When negotiating for a remote position, emphasize your self-discipline, time management skills, and ability to work independently. Highlight your previous remote work experience and showcase results achieved while working remotely. Address concerns the employer might have about communication, collaboration, and productivity by providing examples of your successful remote work practices. Additionally, negotiate clear expectations regarding working hours, communication channels, and availability to establish a strong remote work arrangement.

4. Understanding Cultural Differences:

Strategy: If you're negotiating salary in a multinational company or considering a job in a different country, be mindful of cultural differences. Research the cultural norms around salary negotiations in the specific region. Some cultures value directness and assertiveness, while others may prefer a more indirect and subtle approach. Adapt your negotiation style to align with the cultural expectations of the workplace to ensure effective communication and understanding.

5. Leveraging Industry-Specific Knowledge:

Strategy: Different industries have distinct salary standards and expectations. Research industry-specific salary benchmarks to understand the competitive landscape. Leverage your knowledge of industry trends, certifications, and specialized skills during negotiations. Demonstrate your expertise and how your unique skill set can benefit the organization within the context of the specific industry, reinforcing your value proposition.

6. Emphasizing Work-Life Balance and Well-Being:

Strategy: In today's work environment, work-life balance and employee well-being are increasingly valued. When negotiating salary, consider the overall compensation package, including benefits related to health, mental health, parental leave, and flexible work hours. Emphasize the importance of a healthy work-life balance and how the company's support in this area contributes to your overall job satisfaction and productivity.

Navigating the unique considerations of different work environments requires a nuanced approach to salary negotiations. By understanding the specific demands and expectations of startups, corporations, remote work setups, diverse cultural settings, and industry standards, you can tailor your negotiation strategy effectively. Remember, adapting your approach to each scenario demonstrates your adaptability and strategic thinking, positioning you as a valuable asset in any work environment.

Negotiating a Raise in Your Current Position

Negotiating a raise within your current position is a strategic endeavor that requires preparation, confidence, and effective communication. Whether you're seeking recognition for your contributions, aiming to align your salary with industry standards, or responding to increased responsibilities, negotiating a raise necessitates a thoughtful approach. In this section, we'll explore the essential steps to negotiate a raise successfully within your current role.

1. Prepare a Compelling Case:

Strategy: Before initiating the conversation, gather evidence of your accomplishments, skills, and contributions to the organization. Document specific projects you've completed, improvements you've made, and any additional responsibilities you've taken on. Quantify your achievements wherever possible, showcasing your tangible impact on the company's goals and bottom line. Prepare a strong case that highlights your value to the organization.

2. Research Salary Benchmarks:

Strategy: Research industry-specific salary benchmarks and compare your current salary to the market standards for your role and level of experience. Websites, salary surveys, and industry reports can provide valuable insights. Understanding the prevailing market rates for your position strengthens your negotiating position and helps you set realistic expectations.

3. Schedule a Meeting with Your Supervisor:

Strategy: Request a meeting with your supervisor to discuss your compensation. Choose a time when your supervisor is not preoccupied with urgent matters, ensuring they can focus on your conversation. Clearly express your intention to discuss your performance, achievements, and compensation during the meeting. A scheduled appointment demonstrates your professionalism and allows both parties to prepare for the discussion.

4. Articulate Your Value Proposition:

Strategy: During the meeting, confidently articulate your value proposition. Emphasize your accomplishments, skills, and any additional responsibilities you've shouldered since your last salary review. Use specific examples to illustrate your contributions and how they align with the company's objectives. Convey the positive impact you've had on the organization's success.

5. Be Clear and Assertive:

Strategy: Clearly state your request for a raise and be assertive in your communication. Use confident body language, maintain eye contact, and speak in a calm, composed manner. Clearly articulate the salary increase you are seeking, supported by your research and achievements. Be prepared to negotiate, but also have a minimum acceptable figure in mind that aligns with your financial needs and the market standards.

6. Listen and Respond:

Strategy: Pay attention to your supervisor's response and be receptive to their feedback. Address any concerns they may have and respond thoughtfully to their points. Be open to discussing other forms of compensation, such as additional benefits, bonuses, or professional development opportunities, if a salary increase is not immediately feasible.

7. Follow-Up in Writing:

Strategy: After the meeting, follow up with a concise, professionally written email summarizing the points discussed. Express your appreciation for the opportunity to discuss your compensation and reiterate your key achievements and contributions. Politely restate your request for a raise and the reasons supporting your request. A written follow-up provides a documented record of the conversation and ensures clarity on both sides.

8. Be Prepared for Various Outcomes:

Strategy: Be mentally prepared for different outcomes, including a positive response, a counteroffer, or a temporary delay due to budget constraints. If a raise is not immediately granted, inquire about the possibility of a performance review after a specific period. Stay proactive and continue to excel in your role, reinforcing your value to the organization.

Negotiating a raise within your current position is a testament to your confidence, self-advocacy, and value within the organization. By preparing thoroughly, communicating assertively, and demonstrating your contributions, you position yourself as a proactive, valuable team member deserving of recognition and fair compensation. Remember, effective negotiation is a dialogue, and by presenting a compelling case, you increase your chances of securing the raise you deserve.

Handling Salary Negotiations in Diverse Cultures

Navigating salary negotiations in diverse cultures requires a nuanced understanding of cultural norms, communication styles, and expectations. Cultural differences significantly influence the approach to negotiations, making it essential to adapt your strategies to foster effective communication and build positive relationships. In this section, we'll explore key considerations for handling salary negotiations in diverse cultural contexts.

1. Research Cultural Norms:

Strategy: Conduct thorough research on the cultural norms and practices related to negotiations in the specific country or region you're dealing with. Understand how negotiations are traditionally conducted, the level of formality expected, and the role of hierarchy and authority in decision-making. Knowledge of these cultural nuances forms the foundation for a respectful and culturally sensitive approach.

2. Respect Hierarchy and Authority:

Strategy: In cultures where hierarchy and authority play a significant role, show respect for seniority and authority figures. Address individuals using appropriate titles and honorifics. When negotiating, be mindful of the hierarchical structure within the organization and ensure your communication reflects deference to seniority. Acknowledging authority demonstrates cultural respect and facilitates smoother negotiations.

3. Emphasize Building Relationships:
Strategy: Relationship-building is often highly valued in many cultures. Focus on establishing a genuine, personal connection with your counterparts before diving into the negotiation process. Invest time in small talk, demonstrating genuine interest in their culture, traditions, and experiences. Building rapport fosters trust and paves the way for more open and constructive negotiations.

4. Understand Indirect Communication:
Strategy: In some cultures, direct communication may be perceived as confrontational or impolite. Individuals may use indirect language, subtle cues, or non-verbal communication to convey messages. Pay close attention to non-verbal cues, tone of voice, and facial expressions during negotiations. Be receptive to implied meanings and read between the lines to understand the full context of the conversation.

5. Practice Active Listening:
Strategy: Active listening is essential in cross-cultural negotiations. Demonstrate your attentiveness by

nodding, maintaining eye contact, and paraphrasing to confirm your understanding. Encourage your counterparts to share their perspectives, concerns, and expectations. By actively listening and showing empathy, you build trust and demonstrate your respect for their viewpoints.

6. Adapt Your Negotiation Style:
Strategy: Be adaptable in your negotiation style, tailoring your approach to match the cultural preferences of your counterparts. Some cultures may appreciate assertiveness and directness, while others may value patience, diplomacy, and consensus-building. Strive to strike a balance between your assertiveness and cultural sensitivity, adjusting your style to create a positive and respectful negotiation environment.

7. Be Mindful of Timing:
Strategy: Consider the cultural aspects related to timing, such as holidays, festivals, and significant events. Avoid scheduling negotiations during culturally important days or religious observances, as it may impact the focus and receptiveness of your counterparts. Being aware of the cultural calendar demonstrates your consideration and respect for their traditions and customs.

8. Seek Local Guidance if Necessary:
Strategy: If you are negotiating in a culture significantly different from your own, consider seeking guidance from local experts, consultants, or colleagues familiar with the cultural nuances. Their insights can provide valuable context and help you navigate the negotiation process more effectively. Learning from local experts demonstrates your commitment to understanding and respecting their culture.

9. Express Appreciation and Gratitude:
Strategy: Regardless of the negotiation outcome, express your appreciation and gratitude for the opportunity to engage in the discussion. Send a follow-up message expressing your thanks, regardless of whether an agreement was reached. A gracious and appreciative demeanor leaves a positive impression and fosters goodwill for future interactions.

Navigating salary negotiations in diverse cultures requires cultural intelligence, adaptability, and respect for differences. By understanding and honoring cultural norms, building relationships, practicing active listening, and adapting your communication style, you create an environment conducive to successful negotiations. Embracing cultural diversity enriches your negotiation skills, strengthens global relationships, and enhances your effectiveness in international business contexts.

Chapter 6

Frequently Asked Questions and Troubleshooting

Common Questions and Concerns About Salary Negotiation

Salary negotiation can be a complex and often daunting process, sparking numerous questions and concerns. In this section, we'll address some of the most common queries and uncertainties individuals have about salary negotiation, providing practical answers and solutions to empower you during this critical phase of your career journey.

1. "When is the right time to bring up the topic of salary during the hiring process?"

Answer: The timing of salary discussions varies depending on the company and the specific stage of the hiring process. It's generally advisable to wait until you receive a job offer before discussing salary. However, if the employer initiates the conversation earlier, be prepared to discuss your salary expectations based on your research and the value you bring to the role.

2. "How do I research salary benchmarks for my role and experience level?"

Answer: Utilize online resources, industry-specific websites, salary surveys, and professional organizations to research salary benchmarks. Additionally, reach out to professionals in your network who work in similar roles or industries to gather insights. Comprehensive research will help you establish a reasonable salary range for your negotiation discussions.

3. "What if the employer refuses to negotiate and offers a take-it-or-leave-it salary?"

Answer: If the employer adopts a non-negotiable stance, consider negotiating other aspects of your compensation package, such as additional vacation days, remote work options, professional development opportunities, or bonuses. Alternatively, evaluate the overall package, including benefits and job responsibilities, to determine if it aligns with your career goals and financial needs.

4. "How do I address the topic of salary without sounding greedy or overconfident?"

Answer: Approach the topic of salary with professionalism and confidence. Focus on articulating your values, skills, and achievements that justify your salary expectations. Use data and research to support your request, emphasizing how your contributions will benefit the organization. Be respectful, assertive, and confident in your worth without coming across as arrogant.

5. "What if I receive a counteroffer from my current employer after accepting a job offer elsewhere?"

Answer: Consider the counteroffer carefully and assess whether it addresses the reasons you were exploring new opportunities in the first place. Evaluate not only the financial aspects but also the overall job satisfaction, career growth, and workplace environment. Engage in open communication with both employers, maintaining professionalism and transparency throughout the process.

6. "How do I handle negotiations if I have multiple job offers?"

Answer: When juggling multiple job offers, prioritize the positions based on your career goals, company culture, growth opportunities, and overall fit. Communicate transparently with each employer about your situation, expressing your enthusiasm for the role while being respectful of their timelines. Use your multiple offers as leverage to negotiate the best possible compensation package for your skills and expertise.

7. *"What if the employer asks for my salary expectations? How do I respond?"*

Answer: Provide a salary range based on your research and the industry standards for the role. Be prepared to justify your expectations by highlighting your qualifications, skills, and the value you bring to the position. Express your flexibility and willingness to discuss the compensation package further, emphasizing your focus on finding a mutually beneficial arrangement.

Addressing these common questions and concerns equips you with the knowledge and confidence to navigate salary negotiations effectively. By approaching negotiations with preparation, professionalism, and a positive attitude, you can overcome challenges and advocate for a compensation package that aligns with your skills and contributions. Remember, each negotiation is a unique opportunity to showcase your value and secure a rewarding position in your desired career path.

Troubleshooting and Handling Difficult Scenarios

Navigating salary negotiations can be challenging, especially when faced with unexpected or difficult situations. In this section, we'll address common challenges and provide effective strategies for troubleshooting and handling difficult scenarios during the negotiation process.

1. Handling a Lowball Offer:

Strategy: If you receive a lowball offer significantly below your expectations, express gratitude for the opportunity and professionally counteroffer. Justify your request with research, emphasizing your skills, experience, and industry standards. Be firm but respectful, demonstrating your value while leaving room for negotiation. If the offer remains inadequate, consider whether the overall compensation package, benefits, or growth opportunities offset the lower salary.

2. Responding to a Salary Freeze or Budget Constraints:

Strategy: If the employer cites budget constraints or a salary freeze, express understanding while exploring alternative forms of compensation. Negotiate for additional benefits, such as extra vacation days, professional development opportunities, or performance bonuses. Alternatively, inquire about the possibility of revisiting the salary once the company's financial situation improves. Maintain open communication and express your willingness to collaborate on finding creative solutions.

3. Handling Personal Questions About Current Salary:

Strategy: If the interviewer or employer asks about your current salary, politely deflect the question by focusing on your market value and the salary range you are seeking for the new role. Emphasize your skills, experience, and the contributions you will bring to the organization. Redirect the conversation to the value you will provide in the prospective position, steering away from discussions about your current or previous earnings.

4. Negotiating with a Difficult or Unresponsive Employer:

Strategy: If you encounter a difficult or unresponsive employer, remain patient, professional, and persistent. Send follow-up emails expressing your continued interest in the position and your eagerness to discuss the compensation package further. Be courteous and respectful in your communication, emphasizing your enthusiasm for the role. If the employer remains unresponsive, consider reaching out through alternative channels, such as a different contact person within the organization, to reopen the lines of communication.

5. Handling Counteroffers from Your Current Employer:

Strategy: If your current employer presents a counteroffer after you've accepted a job offer elsewhere, carefully evaluate the offer in light of your reasons for considering a new position. Assess whether the counteroffer addresses the issues that led you to explore other opportunities. Engage in honest and respectful communication with your current employer, expressing gratitude for the counteroffer while clearly stating your reasons for pursuing the new position. Make decisions based on your long-term career goals and overall job satisfaction.

6. Negotiating Benefits and Perks:

Strategy: When negotiating benefits and perks, prioritize what matters most to you, whether it's health insurance, retirement plans, remote work options, or professional development opportunities. Clearly express your preferences and inquire about the company's flexibility in customizing benefits packages. Be open to compromise and creative solutions, focusing on achieving a well-rounded compensation package that aligns with your needs and priorities.

Handling difficult scenarios during salary negotiations requires a combination of assertiveness, flexibility, and professionalism. By staying composed, respectful, and solution-oriented, you can navigate challenges effectively and work toward a mutually beneficial resolution. Remember, effective communication and a positive attitude can often turn a challenging situation into an opportunity for constructive dialogue and successful negotiation.

Conclusion

In the world of software engineering, the path to a better salary is paved with preparation, persistence, and effective negotiation. "How to Negotiate a Better Salary for Software Engineers" has taken you on a journey through the intricate art of securing the compensation you deserve in a competitive industry.

You've learned how to research salary benchmarks, assess your value, and confidently navigate the negotiation process. We've delved into strategies for mastering the art of effective communication, crafting compelling personal pitches, and overcoming common salary negotiation challenges.

From initiating the negotiation to sealing the deal and building lasting relationships, you've discovered the essential steps to enhance your earning potential. You've also gained insights into special considerations for different work environments, handling diverse cultures, and troubleshooting complex scenarios.

As you conclude this book, remember that the knowledge and skills you've acquired are not just theoretical concepts; they are actionable tools that can empower you to make meaningful changes in your career. The journey to a better salary isn't just about the numbers, it's about recognizing your worth, advocating for it, and achieving the financial rewards that reflect your skills and contributions.

May your future salary negotiations be a testament to your confidence, professionalism, and the value you bring to the software engineering industry. Use the wisdom you've gained here to open doors, advance your career, and secure the financial compensation that aligns with your aspirations.

In your pursuit of a better salary, may you not only unlock your earning potential but also embark on a fulfilling and prosperous journey in the dynamic world of software engineering. Your future is limited only by your determination and willingness to apply the strategies and insights provided in this guide. Here's to a successful and lucrative career ahead!

www.ingramcontent.com/pod-product-compliance
Lightning Source LLC
Chambersburg PA
CBHW062351290526
45794CB00005B/2182